Day Dreamer

Gratitude - List the things for which you are thankful today

1_____

_____

2_____

_____

3_____

_____

Affirmations - List positive things about yourself: I Am...

1_____

_____

2_____

_____

3_____

_____

List your current personal or financial goals.

1_____

_____

2_____

_____

3_____

_____

Think of someone for whom you are grateful today:
_____ I am thankful for this person
because_____

_____

Gratitude - List the things for which you are thankful today

1 _____
_____

2 _____
_____

3 _____
_____

Affirmations - List positive things about yourself: I Am...

1 _____
_____

2 _____
_____

3 _____
_____

List your current personal or financial goals.

1 _____
_____

2 _____
_____

3 _____
_____

Think of someone for whom you are grateful today:
_____ I am thankful for this person
because_____
_____

Gratitude - List the things for which you are thankful today

1_____
_____

2_____
_____

3_____
_____

Affirmations - List positive things about yourself: I Am...

1_____
_____

2_____
_____

3_____
_____

List your current personal or financial goals.

1_____
_____

2_____
_____

3_____
_____

Think of someone for whom you are grateful today:
_____ I am thankful for this person
because_____
_____

Gratitude - List the things for which you are thankful today

1 _____
_____

2 _____
_____

3 _____
_____

Affirmations - List positive things about yourself: I Am…

1 _____
_____

2 _____
_____

3 _____
_____

List your current personal or financial goals.

1 _____
_____

2 _____
_____

3 _____
_____

Think of someone for whom you are grateful today:
_____ I am thankful for this person
because _____
_____

Gratitude - List the things for which you are thankful today

1_____
_____

2_____
_____

3_____
_____

Affirmations - List positive things about yourself: I Am...

1_____
_____

2_____
_____

3_____
_____

List your current personal or financial goals.

1_____
_____

2_____
_____

3_____
_____

Think of someone for whom you are grateful today:
_____I am thankful for this person
because_____
_____

Gratitude - List the things for which you are thankful today

1_____

_____

2_____

_____

3_____

_____

Affirmations - List positive things about yourself: I Am...

1_____

_____

2_____

_____

3_____

_____

List your current personal or financial goals.

1_____

_____

2_____

_____

3_____

_____

Think of someone for whom you are grateful today:
_____I am thankful for this person
because_____

_____

Gratitude - List the things for which you are thankful today

1_____
_____

2_____
_____

3_____
_____

Affirmations - List positive things about yourself: I Am…

1_____
_____

2_____
_____

3_____
_____

List your current personal or financial goals.

1_____
_____

2_____
_____

3_____
_____

Think of someone for whom you are grateful today:
_____I am thankful for this person
because_____
_____

Try to list at least 35 specific things for which you are grateful, and briefly explain why.

_____
_____
_____
_____
_____
_____
_____
_____
_____
_____
_____
_____
_____
_____
_____
_____
_____
_____
_____
_____
_____
_____
_____
_____
_____
_____
_____
_____
_____
_____
_____
_____
_____
_____

Gratitude - List the things for which you are thankful today

1_____
_____

2_____
_____

3_____
_____

Affirmations - List positive things about yourself: I Am…

1_____
_____

2_____
_____

3_____
_____

List your current personal or financial goals.

1_____
_____

2_____
_____

3_____
_____

Think of someone for whom you are grateful today:
_____I am thankful for this person
because_____
_____

Gratitude - List the things for which you are thankful today

1_____

_____

2_____

_____

3_____

_____

Affirmations - List positive things about yourself: I Am...

1_____

_____

2_____

_____

3_____

_____

List your current personal or financial goals.

1_____

_____

2_____

_____

3_____

_____

Think of someone for whom you are grateful today:
_____I am thankful for this person
because_____

_____

Gratitude - List the things for which you are thankful today

1_____
_____

2_____
_____

3_____
_____

Affirmations - List positive things about yourself: I Am...

1_____
_____

2_____
_____

3_____
_____

List your current personal or financial goals.

1_____
_____

2_____
_____

3_____
_____

Think of someone for whom you are grateful today:
_____I am thankful for this person
because_____
_____

Gratitude - List the things for which you are thankful today

1 _____

_____

2 _____

_____

3 _____

_____

Affirmations - List positive things about yourself: I Am...

1 _____

_____

2 _____

_____

3 _____

_____

List your current personal or financial goals.

1 _____

_____

2 _____

_____

3 _____

_____

Think of someone for whom you are grateful today:
_____ I am thankful for this person
because_____

_____

Gratitude - List the things for which you are thankful today

1_____
_____

2_____
_____

3_____
_____

Affirmations - List positive things about yourself: I Am…

1_____
_____

2_____
_____

3_____
_____

List your current personal or financial goals.

1_____
_____

2_____
_____

3_____
_____

Think of someone for whom you are grateful today:
_____I am thankful for this person
because_____
_____

Gratitude - List the things for which you are thankful today

1_____
_____

2_____
_____

3_____
_____

Affirmations - List positive things about yourself: I Am...

1_____
_____

2_____
_____

3_____
_____

List your current personal or financial goals.

1_____
_____

2_____
_____

3_____
_____

Think of someone for whom you are grateful today:
_____I am thankful for this person
because_____
_____

Gratitude - List the things for which you are thankful today

1_____

_____

2_____

_____

3_____

_____

Affirmations - List positive things about yourself: I Am…

1_____

_____

2_____

_____

3_____

_____

List your current personal or financial goals.

1_____

_____

2_____

_____

3_____

_____

Think of someone for whom you are grateful today:
_____I am thankful for this person
because_____

_____

List three very specific financial goals.

1 _____

_____

2 _____

_____

3 _____

_____

Explain why you want to achieve each goal and how its achievement will change your life for the better.

1 _____

_____

2 _____

_____

3 _____

_____

List the steps you will take to reach each of these goals.

1 _____

_____

2 _____

_____

3 _____

_____

Gratitude - List the things for which you are thankful today

1 _____
_____

2 _____
_____

3 _____
_____

Affirmations - List positive things about yourself: I Am...

1 _____
_____

2 _____
_____

3 _____
_____

List your current personal or financial goals.

1 _____
_____

2 _____
_____

3 _____
_____

Think of someone for whom you are grateful today:
_____I am thankful for this person
because_____
_____

Gratitude - List the things for which you are thankful today

1 _____

_____

2 _____

_____

3 _____

_____

Affirmations - List positive things about yourself: I Am...

1 _____

_____

2 _____

_____

3 _____

_____

List your current personal or financial goals.

1 _____

_____

2 _____

_____

3 _____

_____

Think of someone for whom you are grateful today:

_____I am thankful for this person

because_____

_____

Gratitude - List the things for which you are thankful today

1_____
_____

2_____
_____

3_____
_____

Affirmations - List positive things about yourself: I Am...

1_____
_____

2_____
_____

3_____
_____

List your current personal or financial goals.

1_____
_____

2_____
_____

3_____
_____

Think of someone for whom you are grateful today:
_____I am thankful for this person
because_____
_____

Gratitude - List the things for which you are thankful today

1_____

_____

2_____

_____

3_____

_____

Affirmations - List positive things about yourself: I Am...

1_____

_____

2_____

_____

3_____

_____

List your current personal or financial goals.

1_____

_____

2_____

_____

3_____

_____

Think of someone for whom you are grateful today:

_____I am thankful for this person

because_____

_____

Gratitude - List the things for which you are thankful today

1_____

_____

2_____

_____

3_____

_____

Affirmations - List positive things about yourself: I Am...

1_____

_____

2_____

_____

3_____

_____

List your current personal or financial goals.

1_____

_____

2_____

_____

3_____

_____

Think of someone for whom you are grateful today:
_____I am thankful for this person
because_____

_____

Gratitude - List the things for which you are thankful today

1_____

_____

2_____

_____

3_____

_____

Affirmations - List positive things about yourself: I Am...

1_____

_____

2_____

_____

3_____

_____

List your current personal or financial goals.

1_____

_____

2_____

_____

3_____

_____

Think of someone for whom you are grateful today:
_____I am thankful for this person
because_____

_____

Gratitude - List the things for which you are thankful today

1_____

_____

2_____

_____

3_____

_____

Affirmations - List positive things about yourself: I Am...

1_____

_____

2_____

_____

3_____

_____

List your current personal or financial goals.

1_____

_____

2_____

_____

3_____

_____

Think of someone for whom you are grateful today:
_____I am thankful for this person
because_____

_____

List your top three goals. Include a target completion date
for each goal.

1_____
_____

2_____
_____

3_____
_____

List how completing each of these goals will enrich your
life.

1_____
_____

2_____
_____

3_____
_____

List the steps that you will need to complete in order to
check each of these goals off your list..

1_____
_____

2_____
_____

3_____
_____

Gratitude - List the things for which you are thankful today

1_____
_____

2_____
_____

3_____
_____

Affirmations - List positive things about yourself: I Am...

1_____
_____

2_____
_____

3_____
_____

List your current personal or financial goals.

1_____
_____

2_____
_____

3_____
_____

Think of someone for whom you are grateful today:
_____I am thankful for this person
because_____
_____

Gratitude - List the things for which you are thankful today

1_____

_____

2_____

_____

3_____

_____

Affirmations - List positive things about yourself: I Am...

1_____

_____

2_____

_____

3_____

_____

List your current personal or financial goals.

1_____

_____

2_____

_____

3_____

_____

Think of someone for whom you are grateful today:
_____I am thankful for this person
because_____

_____

Gratitude - List the things for which you are thankful today

1_____
_____

2_____
_____

3_____
_____

Affirmations - List positive things about yourself: I Am...

1_____
_____

2_____
_____

3_____
_____

List your current personal or financial goals.

1_____
_____

2_____
_____

3_____
_____

Think of someone for whom you are grateful today:
_____ I am thankful for this person
because_____
_____

Gratitude - List the things for which you are thankful today

1 _____
_____

2 _____
_____

3 _____
_____

Affirmations - List positive things about yourself: I Am...

1 _____
_____

2 _____
_____

3 _____
_____

List your current personal or financial goals.

1 _____
_____

2 _____
_____

3 _____
_____

Think of someone for whom you are grateful today:
_____ I am thankful for this person
because _____
_____

Gratitude - List the things for which you are thankful today

1_____
_____

2_____
_____

3_____
_____

Affirmations - List positive things about yourself: I Am...

1_____
_____

2_____
_____

3_____
_____

List your current personal or financial goals.

1_____
_____

2_____
_____

3_____
_____

Think of someone for whom you are grateful today:
_____I am thankful for this person
because_____
_____

Gratitude - List the things for which you are thankful today

1_____
_____

2_____
_____

3_____
_____

Affirmations - List positive things about yourself: I Am…

1_____
_____

2_____
_____

3_____
_____

List your current personal or financial goals.

1_____
_____

2_____
_____

3_____
_____

Think of someone for whom you are grateful today:
_____I am thankful for this person
because_____
_____

Gratitude - List the things for which you are thankful today

1 _____
_____

2 _____
_____

3 _____
_____

Affirmations - List positive things about yourself: I Am...

1 _____
_____

2 _____
_____

3 _____
_____

List your current personal or financial goals.

1 _____
_____

2 _____
_____

3 _____
_____

Think of someone for whom you are grateful today:
_____ I am thankful for this person
because _____
_____

List three things that you can SEE for which you are grateful.

1_____
_____

2_____
_____

3_____
_____

List three things that you can TOUCH for which you are grateful.

1_____
_____

2_____
_____

3_____
_____

List three things that you can SMELL for which you are grateful.

1_____
_____

2_____
_____

3_____
_____

Gratitude - List the things for which you are thankful today

1_____
_____

2_____
_____

3_____
_____

Affirmations - List positive things about yourself: I Am...

1_____
_____

2_____
_____

3_____
_____

List your current personal or financial goals.

1_____
_____

2_____
_____

3_____
_____

Think of someone for whom you are grateful today:
_____I am thankful for this person
because_____
_____

Gratitude - List the things for which you are thankful today

1 _____

_____

2 _____

_____

3 _____

_____

Affirmations - List positive things about yourself: I Am...

1 _____

_____

2 _____

_____

3 _____

_____

List your current personal or financial goals.

1 _____

_____

2 _____

_____

3 _____

_____

Think of someone for whom you are grateful today:

_____I am thankful for this person

because_____

_____

Gratitude - List the things for which you are thankful today

1_____
_____

2_____
_____

3_____
_____

Affirmations - List positive things about yourself: I Am...

1_____
_____

2_____
_____

3_____
_____

List your current personal or financial goals.

1_____
_____

2_____
_____

3_____
_____

Think of someone for whom you are grateful today:
_____I am thankful for this person
because_____
_____

Gratitude - List the things for which you are thankful today

1_____

_____

2_____

_____

3_____

_____

Affirmations - List positive things about yourself: I Am...

1_____

_____

2_____

_____

3_____

_____

List your current personal or financial goals.

1_____

_____

2_____

_____

3_____

_____

Think of someone for whom you are grateful today:

_____I am thankful for this person

because_____

_____

Gratitude - List the things for which you are thankful today

1_____
_____

2_____
_____

3_____
_____

Affirmations - List positive things about yourself: I Am...

1_____
_____

2_____
_____

3_____
_____

List your current personal or financial goals.

1_____
_____

2_____
_____

3_____
_____

Think of someone for whom you are grateful today:
_____I am thankful for this person
because_____
_____

Gratitude - List the things for which you are thankful today

1_____
_____

2_____
_____

3_____
_____

Affirmations - List positive things about yourself: I Am...

1_____
_____

2_____
_____

3_____
_____

List your current personal or financial goals.

1_____
_____

2_____
_____

3_____
_____

Think of someone for whom you are grateful today:
_____I am thankful for this person
because_____
_____

Gratitude - List the things for which you are thankful today

1_____
_____

2_____
_____

3_____
_____

Affirmations - List positive things about yourself: I Am...

1_____
_____

2_____
_____

3_____
_____

List your current personal or financial goals.

1_____
_____

2_____
_____

3_____
_____

Think of someone for whom you are grateful today:
_____I am thankful for this person
because_____

Recall a memory of a time when you were feeling your very best, and write down why. Be specific and note down as many details as you can.

_____
_____
_____
_____
_____
_____
_____
_____
_____
_____

Imagine your life with your personal and financial goals met. Write about that moment as if it was happening right now. Be very specific and include detail. Describe what you see, how you're feeling, what you're wearing.

_____
_____
_____
_____
_____
_____
_____
_____
_____
_____
_____
_____
_____
_____

Gratitude - List the things for which you are thankful today

1 _____
_____

2 _____
_____

3 _____
_____

Affirmations - List positive things about yourself: I Am...

1 _____
_____

2 _____
_____

3 _____
_____

List your current personal or financial goals.

1 _____
_____

2 _____
_____

3 _____
_____

Think of someone for whom you are grateful today:
_____I am thankful for this person
because_____
_____

Gratitude - List the things for which you are thankful today

1_____
_____

2_____
_____

3_____
_____

Affirmations - List positive things about yourself: I Am...

1_____
_____

2_____
_____

3_____
_____

List your current personal or financial goals.

1_____
_____

2_____
_____

3_____
_____

Think of someone for whom you are grateful today:
_____I am thankful for this person
because_____
_____

Gratitude - List the things for which you are thankful today

1_____

_____

2_____

_____

3_____

_____

Affirmations - List positive things about yourself: I Am...

1_____

_____

2_____

_____

3_____

_____

List your current personal or financial goals.

1_____

_____

2_____

_____

3_____

_____

Think of someone for whom you are grateful today:
_____I am thankful for this person
because_____

_____

Gratitude - List the things for which you are thankful today

1_____
_____

2_____
_____

3_____
_____

Affirmations - List positive things about yourself: I Am...

1_____
_____

2_____
_____

3_____
_____

List your current personal or financial goals.

1_____
_____

2_____
_____

3_____
_____

Think of someone for whom you are grateful today:
_____I am thankful for this person
because_____
_____

Gratitude - List the things for which you are thankful today

1_____
_____

2_____
_____

3_____
_____

Affirmations - List positive things about yourself: I Am...

1_____
_____

2_____
_____

3_____
_____

List your current personal or financial goals.

1_____
_____

2_____
_____

3_____
_____

Think of someone for whom you are grateful today:
_____I am thankful for this person
because_____
_____

Gratitude - List the things for which you are thankful today

1 _____
_____

2 _____
_____

3 _____
_____

Affirmations - List positive things about yourself: I Am...

1 _____
_____

2 _____
_____

3 _____
_____

List your current personal or financial goals.

1 _____
_____

2 _____
_____

3 _____
_____

Think of someone for whom you are grateful today:
_____ I am thankful for this person
because _____
_____

Gratitude - List the things for which you are thankful today

1_____

_____

2_____

_____

3_____

_____

Affirmations - List positive things about yourself: I Am...

1_____

_____

2_____

_____

3_____

_____

List your current personal or financial goals.

1_____

_____

2_____

_____

3_____

_____

Think of someone for whom you are grateful today:
_____I am thankful for this person
because_____

_____

Write down three things that someone has told you, or that you have told yourself, that left you discouraged from working on your goals.

1_____

_____

2_____

_____

3_____

_____

Describe exactly what upset you about each comment.

1_____

_____

2_____

_____

3_____

_____

Now write down why each comment is not true.

1_____

_____

2_____

_____

3_____

_____

Gratitude - List the things for which you are thankful today

1_____

_____

2_____

_____

3_____

_____

Affirmations - List positive things about yourself: I Am…

1_____

_____

2_____

_____

3_____

_____

List your current personal or financial goals.

1_____

_____

2_____

_____

3_____

_____

Think of someone for whom you are grateful today:
_____I am thankful for this person
because_____

_____

Gratitude - List the things for which you are thankful today

1 _____
_____

2 _____
_____

3 _____
_____

Affirmations - List positive things about yourself: I Am...

1 _____
_____

2 _____
_____

3 _____
_____

List your current personal or financial goals.

1 _____
_____

2 _____
_____

3 _____
_____

Think of someone for whom you are grateful today:
_____I am thankful for this person
because_____
_____

Gratitude - List the things for which you are thankful today

1_____

_____

2_____

_____

3_____

_____

Affirmations - List positive things about yourself: I Am...

1_____

_____

2_____

_____

3_____

_____

List your current personal or financial goals.

1_____

_____

2_____

_____

3_____

_____

Think of someone for whom you are grateful today:
_____ I am thankful for this person
because_____

_____

Gratitude - List the things for which you are thankful today

1_____
_____

2_____
_____

3_____
_____

Affirmations - List positive things about yourself: I Am…

1_____
_____

2_____
_____

3_____
_____

List your current personal or financial goals.

1_____
_____

2_____
_____

3_____
_____

Think of someone for whom you are grateful today:
_____I am thankful for this person
because_____
_____

Gratitude - List the things for which you are thankful today

1 _____
_____

2 _____
_____

3 _____
_____

Affirmations - List positive things about yourself: I Am…

1 _____
_____

2 _____
_____

3 _____
_____

List your current personal or financial goals.

1 _____
_____

2 _____
_____

3 _____
_____

Think of someone for whom you are grateful today:
_____ I am thankful for this person
because_____
_____

Gratitude - List the things for which you are thankful today

1 _____
_____

2 _____
_____

3 _____
_____

Affirmations - List positive things about yourself: I Am...

1 _____
_____

2 _____
_____

3 _____
_____

List your current personal or financial goals.

1 _____
_____

2 _____
_____

3 _____
_____

Think of someone for whom you are grateful today:
_____ I am thankful for this person
because _____
_____

Gratitude - List the things for which you are thankful today

1_____
_____

2_____
_____

3_____
_____

Affirmations - List positive things about yourself: I Am…

1_____
_____

2_____
_____

3_____
_____

List your current personal or financial goals.

1_____
_____

2_____
_____

3_____
_____

Think of someone for whom you are grateful today:
_____I am thankful for this person
because_____
_____

List three people whom you admire.

_____
_____
_____

Think about the wonderful qualities these three people possess, and why you admire them. Imagine yourself possessing these same qualities. List each quality as a personal affirmation: "I am creative."

_____
_____
_____
_____
_____
_____
_____
_____
_____
_____
_____
_____
_____
_____
_____
_____
_____
_____
_____
_____
_____
_____

Gratitude - List the things for which you are thankful today

1_____
_____

2_____
_____

3_____
_____

Affirmations - List positive things about yourself: I Am…

1_____
_____

2_____
_____

3_____
_____

List your current personal or financial goals.

1_____
_____

2_____
_____

3_____
_____

Think of someone for whom you are grateful today:
_____I am thankful for this person
because_____
_____

Gratitude - List the things for which you are thankful today

1_____
_____

2_____
_____

3_____
_____

Affirmations - List positive things about yourself: I Am...

1_____
_____

2_____
_____

3_____
_____

List your current personal or financial goals.

1_____
_____

2_____
_____

3_____
_____

Think of someone for whom you are grateful today:
_____I am thankful for this person
because_____
_____

Gratitude - List the things for which you are thankful today

1_____
_____

2_____
_____

3_____
_____

Affirmations - List positive things about yourself: I Am…

1_____
_____

2_____
_____

3_____
_____

List your current personal or financial goals.

1_____
_____

2_____
_____

3_____
_____

Think of someone for whom you are grateful today:
_____I am thankful for this person
because_____
_____

Gratitude - List the things for which you are thankful today

1 _____

2 _____

3 _____

Affirmations - List positive things about yourself: I Am...

1 _____

2 _____

3 _____

List your current personal or financial goals.

1 _____

2 _____

3 _____

Think of someone for whom you are grateful today:
_____ I am thankful for this person
because _____

_____

Gratitude - List the things for which you are thankful today

1 _____
_____

2 _____
_____

3 _____
_____

Affirmations - List positive things about yourself: I Am...

1 _____
_____

2 _____
_____

3 _____
_____

List your current personal or financial goals.

1 _____
_____

2 _____
_____

3 _____
_____

Think of someone for whom you are grateful today:
_____ I am thankful for this person
because _____

_____

Gratitude - List the things for which you are thankful today

1_____
_____

2_____
_____

3_____
_____

Affirmations - List positive things about yourself: I Am...

1_____
_____

2_____
_____

3_____
_____

List your current personal or financial goals.

1_____
_____

2_____
_____

3_____
_____

Think of someone for whom you are grateful today:
_____I am thankful for this person
because_____
_____

Gratitude - List the things for which you are thankful today

1_____
_____

2_____
_____

3_____
_____

Affirmations - List positive things about yourself: I Am...

1_____
_____

2_____
_____

3_____
_____

List your current personal or financial goals.

1_____
_____

2_____
_____

3_____
_____

Think of someone for whom you are grateful today:
_____I am thankful for this person
because_____
_____

Write down all of the things for which you are grateful. Dig deep and be specific. Include people, smells, feelings, sounds, tastes, things you've witnessed, and goals.

_____
_____
_____
_____
_____
_____
_____
_____
_____
_____
_____
_____
_____
_____
_____
_____
_____
_____
_____
_____
_____
_____
_____
_____
_____
_____
_____
_____
_____

Made in the USA
San Bernardino, CA
10 October 2017